5 ETUDES
FOR SOLO GUITAR

by DAVE ISAACS

www.NashvilleGuitarGuru.com

ISBN (ebook): 978-0-578-76462-7
ISBN (print): 978-0-578-76604-1
Printed in USA
Illustrations and book design: Christa Schoenbrodt, Studio Haus
Back page photo: Andy Ellis

5 ETUDES
FOR SOLO GUITAR
by DAVE ISAACS

THOUGHTS ON PRACTICING

There's no single "best" way to organize your practice time. Deliberate work of any kind is always going to be productive. But to play any piece of music well, your learning process has to go through three stages:

1. Learning the notes (knowledge of the music)

2. Strengthening the execution (technical accuracy)

3. Developing the flow (fluidity in execution)

Learning the notes means more than following along with the page. Get to know the music so well that every element is familiar, and leave the surprises for the audience.

Strengthen execution by identifying and solving technical problems. If you repeatedly miss a change, there's a specific mechanical reason. Find it and you solve the problem.

Developing flow means you can play the song from beginning to end confidently. That doesn't mean you might not make mistakes, but they won't interrupt your performance – in fact, your audience might never notice.

As you work, you can break things down to smaller elements at any moment when a problem presents itself. Sometimes an issue might come up during your flow practice that requires a return to detailed technique work. Don't view this as a step back but forward: polishing a detail you hadn't previously seen, or reinforcing something that hadn't quite locked in yet.

Practicing is circular as well as linear, and every time you cycle back around you will discover and improve something you may have missed before. Viewing practice as an open-ended process like this helps keep your progress in perspective: mastery is relative, so simply aim for today's best.

PRACTICE NOTES

PERFORMANCE NOTES

These Etudes were written specifically to develop thumb-finger coordination, and may be played finger-style or with a pick-and-fingers hybrid technique.

ETUDE 1

All grace notes are played on the beat.

The melody is in the bass (the lowest sounding note of each chord) throughout the A section, measures 1-16 and 25-30. Play all bass notes with the thumb, with the fingers filling in the higher strings. The melody is in the top voice (highest sounding notes) in the B section (measures 17-24) and outro (measures 32-37).

The octave harmonics in measures 35-37 are played by touching the note in brackets with the plucking hand index finger, directly over the fret. While the fingertip is touching, pluck the string with the ring finger of the same hand.

ETUDE 2

This is a variation on a "Travis pick" pattern in that the thumb drives the beat and often alternates strings. Use the picking hand thumb for the bass strings, and the remaining fingers (index, middle, ring) to pluck the trebles.

ETUDE 3

Bring out the bass strings with the picking hand thumb. In measures 14-22 and 39-53, pluck the 3-note chords with thumb-index-middle or thumb-middle-ring.

Be sure to play the slurs (hammer-ons and pull-offs) in time. Observe the note values and don't let them interrupt the flow of the rhythm.

ETUDE 4

This melody is played as an arpeggio, alternating between the plucking hand thumb and finger alternately. Note the 6/8 rhythm.

The natural harmonics in the intro are played by touching the fret hand finger lightly to the string directly over the fret, rather than just behind it as you ordinarily would. Use an extended fret hand finger as if you were going to play a barre. Touch the string but don't hold it down, and lift the fret hand finger immediately after you pluck.

ETUDE 5

The melody begins on the second note, and continues with a syncopated rhythm between the steady pulse established by the thumb. As before, use the thumb for notes on strings 4, 5, and 6.

In the B section, the melody is played with the thumb on the 4th and 3rd strings.

1
IN C MAJOR

All grace notes are played on the beat. | The melody is in the bass (the lowest sounding note of each chord) throughout the A section, measures 1-16 and 25-30. Play all bass notes with the thumb, with the fingers filling in the higher strings. The melody is in the top voice (highest sounding notes) in the B section (measures 17-24) and outro (measures 32-37). | The octave harmonics in measures 35-37 are played by touching the note in brackets with the plucking hand index finger, directly over the fret. While the fingertip is touching, pluck the string with the ring finger of the same hand.

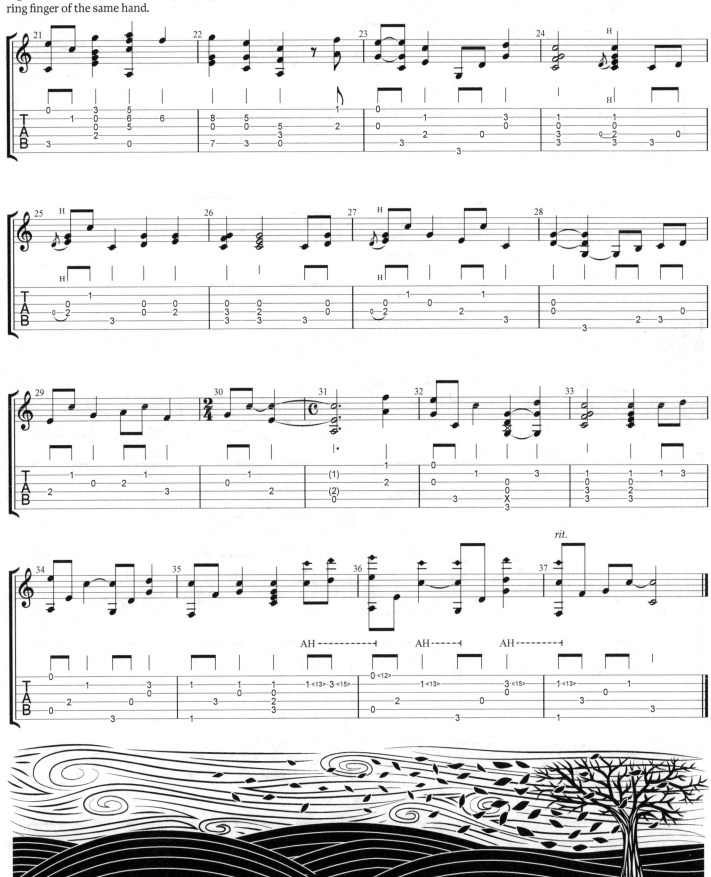

2
IN G MAJOR

This is a variation on a "Travis pick" pattern in that the thumb drives the beat and often alternates strings. Use the picking hand thumb for the bass strings, and the remaining fingers (index, middle, ring) to pluck the trebles.

3
IN A MINOR

Bring out the bass strings with the picking hand thumb. In measures 14-22 and 39-53, pluck the 3-note chords with thumb-index-middle or thumb-middle-ring. | Be sure to play the slurs (hammer-ons and pull-offs) in time. Observe the note values and don't let them interrupt the flow of the rhythm.

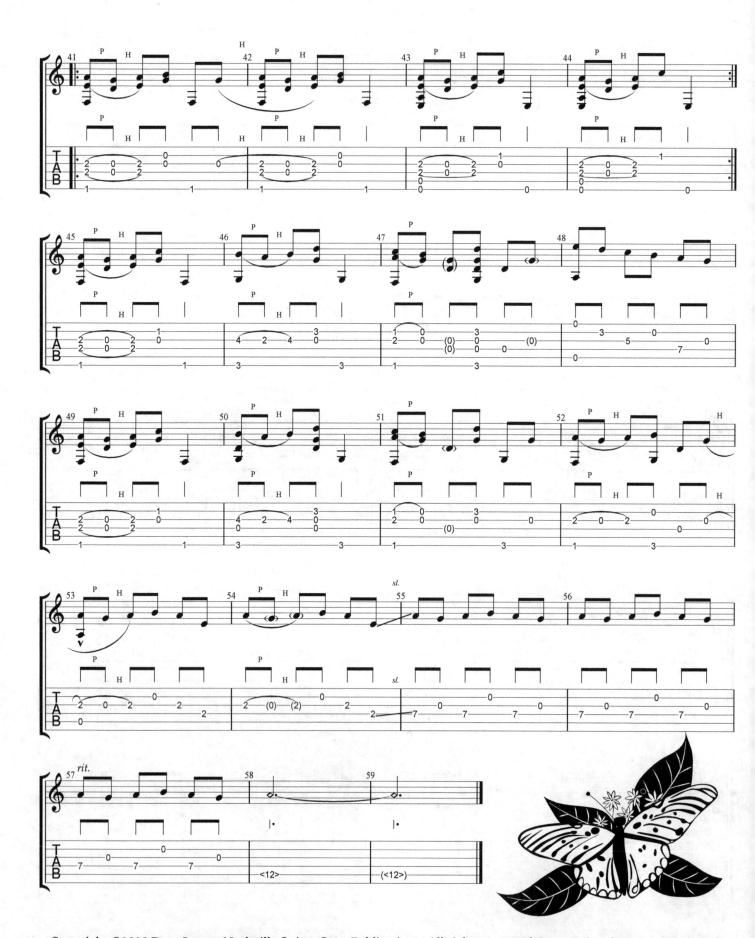

4

IN E MINOR

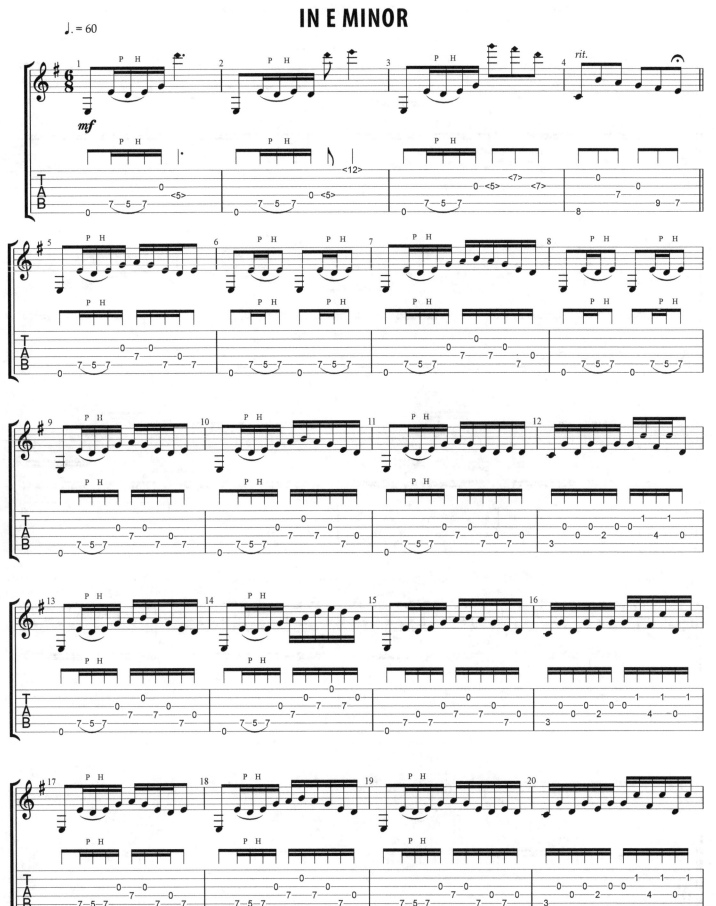

This melody is played as an arpeggio, alternating between the plucking hand thumb and finger alternately. Note the 6/8 rhythm. | The natural harmonics in the intro are played by touching the fret hand finger lightly to the string directly over the fret, rather than just behind it as you ordinarily would. Use an extended fret hand finger as if you were going to play a barre. Touch the string but don't hold it down, and lift the fret hand finger immediately after you pluck.

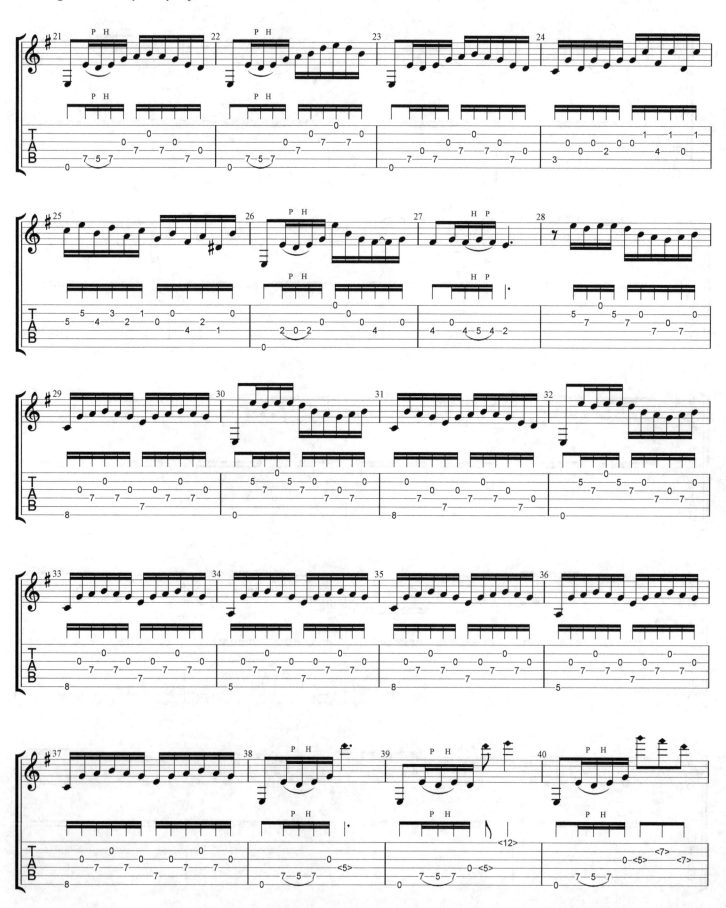

5
IN A MAJOR

The melody begins on the second note, and continues with a syncopated rhythm between the steady pulse established by the thumb. As before, use the thumb for notes on strings 4, 5, and 6. | In the B section, the melody is played with the thumb on the 4th and 3rd strings.

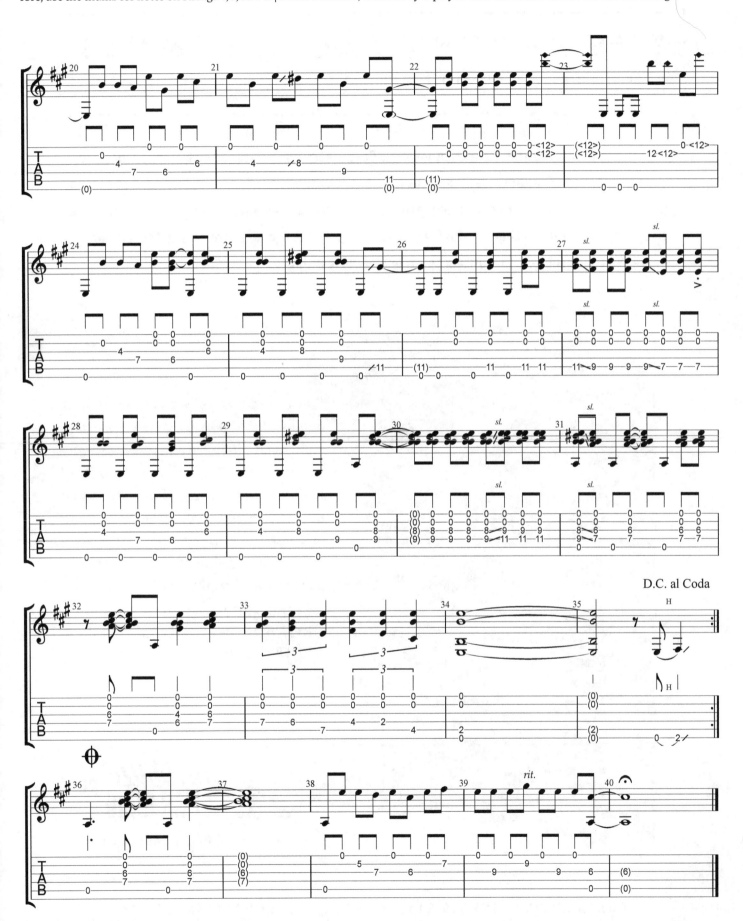

D.C. al Coda

CPSIA information can be obtained
at www.ICGtesting.com
Printed in the USA
LVHW061621191120
671608LV00008BB/292